of emigration from

AFRICA

Catherine Chambers

FRANKLIN WATTS

A Division of Grolier Publishing

NEW YORK  • SYDNEY

For Mr Hubert, with respect

© Franklin Watts 1996

First American Edition 1997 by
Franklin Watts
A Division of Grolier Publishing Co., Inc.
Sherman Turnpike
Danbury, CT 06813

Library of Congress Cataloging-in-Publication Data
Chambers, Catherine.
     Africa / Catherine Chambers.
          p. cm, —(Origins)
     Includes index.
     Summary: Discusses the origin of this
     huge continent of contrasts, the
     emigration of its inhabitants throughout
     the world, and the role of slavery in the
     lives of its people.
     ISBN 0-531-14416-X
     1. Africa—History—Juvenile literature.
     2. Slavery—History—Juvenile literature.
     3. African diaspora—History—Juvenile
     literature. [1. Africa—History. 2.
     Slavery—History. 3. Africa—Emigration
      and immeigration.] I. Title. II. Series:
     Origins (New York, N.Y.)
     DT22.C47 1997   96-1723
     960—dc20   CIP AC

Series editor: Rachel Cooke
Designer: Simon Borrough
Picture research: Brooks Krikler Resarch

Printed in Malaysia

Picture acknowledgements
t=top; b=bottom; m=middle; r=right; l=left
Mary Evans Picture Library pp. 3, 8, 9t, 10t,
11(t and b), 12b, 13t, 14(t and b), 18(t and b),
21b, 22b, 26r
Robert Harding Picture Library pp. 4, 5t, 21t,
26l, 27t, 28t, 29b
Werner Forman Archive p. 5t
Medimage/Anthony King pp. 6(t and b), 7b, 9m
The Hutchison Library pp. 7t, 10b, 12t, 20,
22t, 27b
A.K.G. London p.9r
Panos Picture Library pp. 13b, 15b, 29t
Frank Spooner Pictures pp. 16t, 19r,
23(lt and lb), 25b
Hulton Getty Collection pp. 16b, 17t, 28b
Corbis Range Collection pp. 17b, 28rb
Spectrum Colour Library p.19l
p.25t Picture supplied by Tate Gallery
Publications © Succession Picasso/Dacs 1996

Contents

What Is Africa?

How do we know that a musical rhythm or a mathematical pattern, a painting or a cooking pot originally came from such a vast land?

Africa is a huge continent with hot dry deserts and tall snowy peaks – with thick tropical forests and open grassy plains. The long Nile River slides up the eastern side; the great Niger River curls around the west.

The contrasts in Africa's peoples and politics are as great as the land and climate. At times, great civilizations have grown up and powerful empires arisen. In contrast, small, self-sufficient communities also emerged in the dense Cameroon and Congo forests or on the deserts of the southwest, where they still live today. City dwellers, villagers, and nomads have all occupied this vast territory, which is believed to be the home of mankind itself.

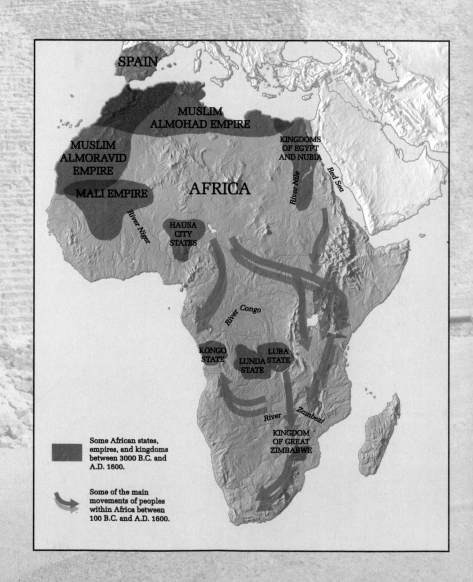

SPAIN

MUSLIM ALMOHAD EMPIRE

MUSLIM ALMORAVID EMPIRE

KINGDOMS OF EGYPT AND NUBIA

MALI EMPIRE

AFRICA

River Nile

Red Sea

River Niger

HAUSA CITY STATES

River Congo

KONGO STATE

LUNDA STATE

LUBA STATE

River Zambezi

KINGDOM OF GREAT ZIMBABWE

Some African states, empires, and kingdoms between 3000 B.C. and A.D. 1600.

Some of the main movements of peoples within Africa between 100 B.C. and A.D. 1600.

Leaving Africa

Over the last 1,400 years, millions of Africans have left their home continent: sometimes as conquerors but more often as slaves. The lives of these Africans changed with each new situation. Mostly, their daily routines were shaped by their new rulers and different environments.

But Africans brought with them their cultures: their beliefs, lifestyles, and customs. They clung to these in strange lands, adapting and developing them to fit their new circumstances. Today it is possible to identify African objects and ideas in far-off lands, even if they were first brought from Africa hundreds of years ago.

The African Identity

But how can we identify something as African when it is found thousands of miles from the African continent? How do we know that a musical rhythm or a mathematical pattern, a painting or a cooking pot originally came from such a vast land? Africa has such enormous contrasts that it is difficult to see it as a single unit with one identity. And, of course, it is not a single unit, nor does it have just one identity – no more than Europe, Asia, or America.

But similar patterns and forms of technology, social and political organization, and religious belief can be found throughout much of Africa. They were spread and exchanged over thousands of years by travelers who cut across Africa in all directions along ancient migration pathways and trade routes. The strongest ideas were taken up by many African communities. So there are certain shapes, rhythms, stories, and ideas that firmly say, "We come from Africa." The movement of people out of Africa introduced these unique African elements to the rest of the world.

◀ To the far left, the soaring pyramids of Giza stand as some of the greatest monuments to African civilizations. Left inset, this ivory mask belonged to the Oba (king) of the great kingdom of Benin, a later African civilization, in the 16th century. Portuguese traders' heads decorate the top.

▼ The richness of African decorative art is shown on this Maasai woman from Kenya. Highly colored, elaborate beadwork can be found from East Africa all the way down to South Africa. Similar color combinations and patterns have been used by Africans in the Americas.

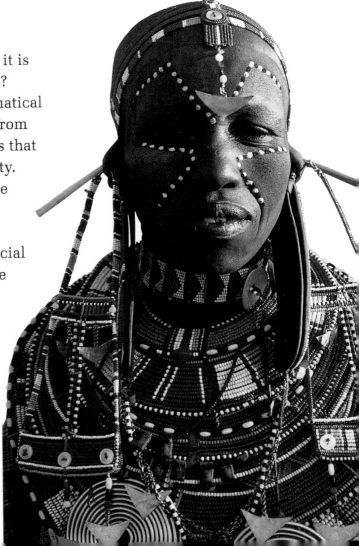

The African Conquerors

In the 7th century A.D., the Holy Prophet Mohammed (PBUH) had established the faith of Islam in the Middle East. By the 8th century, Bedouin nomads had taken it across North Africa. Here, the new religion jostled with existing African cultures and mixed with Jewish, ancient Nubian, and the more modern Greek and Christian Carthaginian lifestyles. Out of this melting pot came an explosive Islamic culture known as Moorish, which had begun and developed in Africa.

As successful Islamic states flourished throughout North Africa, their Moorish rulers felt encouraged to spread the Islamic faith and their own power into southern Europe. In A.D. 711 a fleet of ships sailed across the narrow strip of water that separates Spain from Africa. A Moorish army, inspired by the new religion of Islam, was on its way to Europe.

▲ **From Tarifa in Spain you can see the rocks of Morocco on a clear day. If you had been looking on such a day in A.D. 711, you might have seen the fleet of Moorish ships on its way to conquer Europe in the name of Islam.**

The Moorish Revolution

From the city of Córdoba in southern Spain, a great Islamic empire spread as far west as modern-day Portugal, and north to the Pyrenees. Today, the magnificent palaces and small private courtyards of ordinary homes show the great impact of this empire.

Córdoba was its political, intellectual, and cultural capital, with free schools for the poor, universities, public libraries, and hospitals. Many of the roots of modern mathematics, medicine, and science began here. Irrigation systems, public baths, and water gardens created green and blossoming surroundings. The city even attracted admiring visitors from Arabia, the birthplace of Islam.

▲ Elderly women in Spain and Portugual often dress in dark clothes which cover their bodies well, like these women in southern Spain. The influence of Muslim traditions in women's dress can be seen in this style of clothing.

▼ The three plates are all designed according to the rules of Moorish art. But only the large plate comes from an Islamic country, Morocco. The one next to it comes from Spain, and the top one from Portugal.

The Decline of the Moors

Over the next 500 years, power struggles in the Islamic world led to the Moorish empire splitting up and changing hands. But although this weakened the Moors' hold on Spain, the biggest threat came from Christian armies from the north. Córdoba finally fell in 1236 to the Christian king, Ferdinand III. The remaining power of the Moors then switched to the city of Granada, which survived for a further 200 years until the whole of the Islamic empire gave way to a Christian kingdom in 1491.

Before the Moors were all expelled in 1570, they left behind more than just spectacular buildings and higher learning. Ordinary people, too, had come here from Africa. They had brought with them ordinary everyday things — a style of clothing and cooking, pots, pans, and plates, musical instruments, building methods and tools to make them with. And they introduced new Arabic words to describe these things. Hundreds of these words are still used in Spanish and Portuguese today.

◄ Delicate plasterwork decorates the Alhambra palace in Granada, Spain. Its Moorish motifs include Arabic lettering, leaf and cone shapes, scrolls and geometric patterning.

Sold into Slavery

Between the 15th and the 19th centuries, millions of African slaves were transported across the Atlantic Ocean to the Americas.

Europe soon forgot the African Moors' contribution to their culture. Christian Spain did not want to remember its Islamic past. It is perhaps not surprising that few Spanish Christians stood up for the Moors when they became some of the first victims of the transatlantic slave trade.

Between the 15th and 19th centuries, millions of African slaves were transported across the Atlantic Ocean to the Americas. Here, there grew the biggest settlements of Africans outside Africa. This transatlantic trade was enormous, but it was not the beginning of slavery itself.

An Ancient Trade

The use of slaves has been part of trade and commerce in many areas of the world for thousands of years. In Africa, slaves had been employed from the early empires of Egypt and Kush in the east, to the great Sudanic kingdoms of the grasslands in the west. With the coming of Islam, slaves were transported from Africa to northern Moorish states, the Middle East, and even as far east as Pakistan. But the transatlantic trade was bigger and more brutal than any other slave trade in history. It is difficult to get an exact figure of the numbers of African slaves involved, but 20 million would not be too high.

Slavery existed in Africa before the transatlantic trade, and slave markets continued there even toward its end. This market flourished in Khartoum, Sudan, in the 1870s. Many of these slaves were carried northward and eastward to Islamic kingdoms.

Europe Finds America

In 1492, the Spanish first landed on the islands of the West Indies off Central America under the command of Christopher Columbus. The whole "discovery" was rather an accident, for Columbus was really looking for a new route to the riches of the East, especially India.

Other explorers followed. They discovered great American Indian empires and enormous wealth in gold and silver and vast expanses of land. The American Indian empires were soon crushed as Europeans fought each other for the riches of the islands and the American mainland.

Over the next 200 years, Spain secured much of South America and some of the islands of the West Indies. Portugal gained Brazil, and England and France staked claims in North America, and most of the rest of the West Indies. These European powers sought gold and other minerals and fertile land for tobacco, cotton, and sugar plantations. They had to build towns for the merchants and mining organizers to live in and ports for ships that took the riches back to Europe. All this required labor and a lot of it.

Slaves For a "New World"?

At first, the new rulers used local American Indians and workers shipped out from Europe. But diseases, before unknown to the American Indians, all but wiped them out. Heat, sickness, and harsh working conditions discouraged the Europeans. So, although the slave trade was at this time illegal, a few slave ships transported kidnapped Africans, mainly from West Africa, across the Atlantic Ocean to the Americas. The slave trade had begun.

It was very different from anything Africa had experienced before. Slaves in traditional West African

◄ his engraving shows Columbus landing on San Salvador Island in 1492. Gifts are exchanged with the American Indians. The cross shows Spain's wish to bring Christianity to the Americas.

▲ This altar in the Cathedral of Santa Maria in Seville, Spain, is covered in gold brought from the Americas.

► A 16th-century bronze sculpture from Benin, West Africa, of a Portuguese soldier.

society were often captured in warfare or kidnapped. But after their seizure, African slaves mostly were treated well. In time, they became accepted members of their captors' society.

This account of slavery in Africa was written in 1785 by Olaudah Equiano, who was kidnapped by slavers and taken to the West Indies, where he eventually bought his freedom.

Those prisoners [of war] which were not redeemed or sold we kept as slaves: but how different was their condition from that of the slaves in the [West Indies]! With us [in Africa] they do no more work than other members of the community, even their master; their food, clothing, and lodging, were nearly the same as theirs.

The Changing Slave Trade

The demand of slaves by Europeans changed African slavery completely – capturing slaves was now big business. It got worse in the 17th century when it was discovered that sugar cane grew well in the West Indies, but growing it involved a huge number of workers.

In exchange for goods such as guns, cloth, and ceramics, West African traders and rulers now supplied a constant flow of kidnapped slaves to eager white slave owners. In Central Africa, the Portuguese and Spanish themselves organized capture. Later, in East Africa, traders from the coast raided the interior for their European buyers. There were few areas of the continent that were not touched by the trade.

▲ **Slave hunters often burned down villages to force their inhabitants out into the open, easing capture. This 19th-century scene took place in West Africa.**

▼ **Elmina Castle in Ghana still stands as a reminder of the Portuguese presence in West Africa. This fortress, built in 1482, first protected Portugal's gold trade with Ghana. Later, the fort became a bleak symbol of the slave trade.**

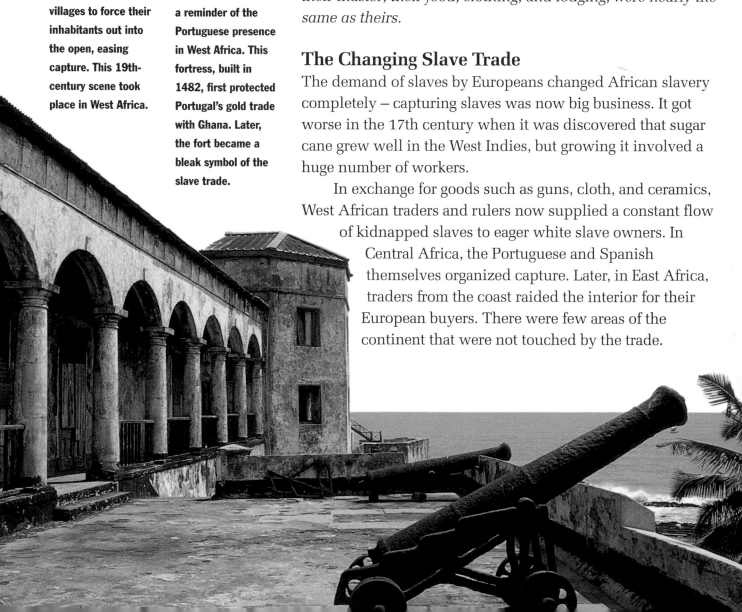

The Longest Journey

Africans taken in a raid were chained at the ankles or shackled around the neck before the long journey to the coast, where busy slave ports had grown. Under the looming fortresses built by the Europeans to protect their trade, the fittest slaves were bundled onto slave ships for their next part of the journey, known as the deadly "middle passage."

The ships were designed to pack in as many people as possible, so, with little room to move, the slaves were held below deck, sometimes in chains, for many weeks. Food and sanitation were poor, and many died of disease even before they reached the Americas.

At the end of the journey, these Africans, still in chains, were lined up on the slave docks and bought as plantation labor or as domestic servants in large houses. Some were sold to buyers from other parts of the Americas.

▲ **This is how African people were packed into the *Brookes*, a slave ship from Liverpool in England. It is no wonder that many died in such conditions. These diagrams were used as evidence against slavery in the 1790s.**

Below deck on a ▶ slave ship, there was no room even to stretch out into a sleeping position. Slaves had to use each others' bodies as pillows.

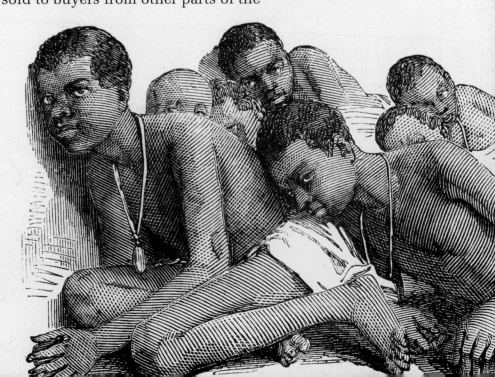

Working Lives

The power of white Americans led to the humiliation and oppression of African-Americans long after the end of slavery.

▼ This advertisement caricatures and exploits Africans. It is typical of the racist attitude toward them even after the end of slavery.

A sugar-plantation ▶ owner built this beautiful house in Barbados on the profits of slave labor.

There was little difference between the daily life of a slave in the West Indies, or one in South America or North America. Life was brutal for nearly all of them. But in each of the these areas, there was a slightly different overall picture.

The West Indies

In the West Indies, most African slaves worked in the rural areas on plantations. Domestic slaves served in grand houses on the estates, looking after the plantation owners and their families. But small numbers of slaves had been freed during island wars between different European nations. Others had bought their freedom. These people, from quite early on, settled in towns. Many became assistants to all kinds of workers, from carpenters and blacksmiths to storekeepers and merchants. Whatever their kind of work, Africans soon outnumbered Europeans on these islands, which made them different from the rest of the Americas.

▲ Picking cotton hurts the hands. But these people had to pick for at least twelve hours a day. The cotton from America's deep South was shipped to Britain where it fed the booming textile industry.

▼ A Venezuelan miner works the silver seams on a bare rock face. Nowadays, he is paid for his work, although probably not much. But for hundreds of years, unpaid slaves did all the work.

North America

Tobacco planters first brought African slaves to Jamestown in Virginia as late as 1619. It was soon discovered that another valuable crop, cotton, could grow well in the hot, humid weather of the southern area and the demand for slaves grew even larger.

The European settlers soon felt American and declared their independence from Britain in 1776. They had always had more control over slaves than elsewhere in the New World. In the southern states, the newly independent Americans defended their tight control over them. Owners often refused slaves permission to marry and many tried to "breed" slave children with what they considered to be "strong" slave women. The power of white Americans led to the humiliation and oppression of African-Americans long after the end of slavery.

South America

In South America, slaves worked not only on plantations, but also in gold and silver mines, in timber forests, and on vast cattle ranches. Africans worked alongside American Indians. Europeans who were born in South America began to mix with both the African and the American Indian populations. While this did not alter the work of slaves, it gave South American culture a different, more multiracial character from that of North America.

▲ A "for sale" advertisement in the Jamaica *Royal Gazette*, 1826, shows Quasheba, a young African woman. She has been branded with a hot iron on her chest and shoulder to show she is a slave.

▲ In the city of Rio de Janeiro in Brazil, slaves are being sold in a shop. They are clearly suffering from malnutrition. This picture was drawn in the 18th century, but slavery continued in Brazil until 1888.

Making Money

The set of accounts below shows how a plantation owner in the 1650s could make a healthy profit by using slaves (here called Negroes). It also gives some clues about the lives of slaves in the Americas.

	£	s	d
We will allow yearly to issue out of profits that arise upon the plantation	500	00	00
As also for the moderate decay of our Negroes, horses and cattle, notwithstanding all our recruits by breeding all these kinds	500	00	00
For foreign provisions of victuals for our servants and some of our slaves, we will allow yearly	100	00	00
For wages to our principal overseer yearly	50	00	00
The charge of clothing the five subordinate overseers yearly	27	05	00
Clothing the remaining men-servants yearly	58	16	00
Clothing four women servants that attend in the house	19	4	00
The remaining six women that do the common work abroad in the fields	21	06	00
The charging of thirty rug gowns for these thirty servants	37	10	00
The clothing of fifty men Negroes	15	00	00
The clothing of fifty women Negroes	20	00	00
Sum total of the expenses is	1,349	01	00
Sum total of the yearly profits of the plantation	8,866	00	00
So the clear profit of this plantation of 500 acres of land amounts to yearly	7,516	00	00

Taken from *History of Barbados* by Ligon, 1657

Note: £=pound sterling, s=shillings (there were 20 shillings in a pound sterling), d=pence (there were 12 pence to a shilling). At this time, you could buy a two-course meal for one shilling in a London restaurant. The plantation owner could have bought 150,739 meals with his profits!

The living conditions of cotton-pickers in Arkansas didn't change very much even after the end of slavery when this picture was taken. Slave children received little education from their owners, but were often self-taught.

In a market in Kingston, Jamaica, today you can see foods that are cooked in Africa as well as the Americas. At the front there are onions, yams, sweet potatoes, and pumpkins.

You can see that the plantation owner spent nearly as much clothing four women servants as he did fifty slaves. He spent some money importing victuals (food) for his servants and for some of his slaves. The rest, who were the majority, were given basic provisions, such as salted meat and pickled fish, sugar, and rum. Slaves themselves grew crops such as yams, plantain, and okra, on plots of land supplied by the plantation owner. As you can see from the accounts, only the overseers (supervisors) received wages. There is no mention of money spent on housing, which for slaves would have been wooden huts with thatched roofs.

But perhaps the most startling item in the accounts is the second one. Here, the owner allows money to replace the slaves, horses, and cattle that "decay," or fall sick and die. Human beings were owned. They were bought, sold, treated, and replaced in exactly the same way as animals.

▲ It takes a lot of back-breaking work to cut a field of sugarcane like this one on the island of Haiti in the West Indies.

▼ By the 1800s, cartoonists in Europe and America were showing the horrors of slavery that had already existed for 300 years.

Working Till They Drop

In this next piece, written later in 1807, the author, Renny, describes the working lives of slaves on a West Indian sugar plantation.

On plantations, the slaves are generally divided into three classes, called gangs; the first of which consists of the most healthy and robust, both of males and females, whose chief business it is, before crop-time, to clear, hole, and plant the ground; and during crop-time to cut the canes, feed the mills, and attend to the manufacture of the sugar... The second gang is composed of young boys and girls, pregnant females, and convalescents [those recovering from an illness], who are chiefly employed in weeding the canes, and other light work...; and the third gang consists of young children, attended by a careful old woman, who are employed in collecting green-meat for the pigs and sheep... They do not, in general, [work] longer than ten hours every day.... In the crop season, however, the arrangement is different; at that time such of the Negroes as are employed in the mill, and boiling houses, often work late, frequently all night; but, in this case, they are commonly divided into watches which relieve each other.

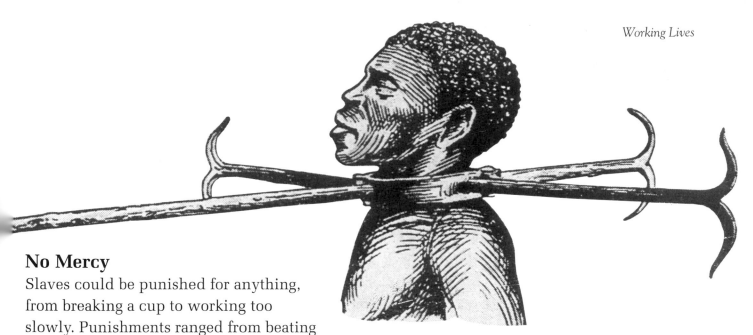

No Mercy

Slaves could be punished for anything, from breaking a cup to working too slowly. Punishments ranged from beating to hanging. This description of the punishment of plantation workers in Jamaica was written in 1707. Most slaves were punished like this at some time in their lives.

For running away, they put iron rings of great weight on their ankles, or pothooks about their necks, which are iron rings with two long necks riveted to them...

For negligence [poor work] they are usually whipped by the overseers with laice-wood switches till they be bloody and several of the switches broken, being first tied up by their hands in the mill-houses.

One of the greatest fears was being late for work. Solomon Northrup, a slave from North America, described the end of a typical day for slaves in the cotton fields:

Finally, at a late hour, they reach the quarters, sleepy and overcome with the long day's toil. Then ... a supper, and dinner for the next day in the field prepared... By this time it is usually midnight. The same fear of punishment... possesses them again on lying down to get a snatch of rest. It is the fear of oversleeping in the morning. Such an offense would certainly be attended with twenty lashes.

With their every move so controlled and restricted, what was left of African life for these people, whose family ways, cultures, and customs seemed so destroyed?

▲ **A neck ring was used to punish and to stop slaves from escaping. Many slaves stood up to their owners or tried to escape.**

▼ **This photograph of five generations of one family was taken in the 1890s. They all lived on the same plantation in South Carolina, before and after slavery's end.**

17

Holding On

It was difficult for African slaves to keep their identities. For a start, Africans from different areas and language groups were mixed together. This meant that Africans lost fluency in their own languages.

In the same way, many of the fine details of separate African cultures disappeared. But the strong features they held in common lived on.

In some places, skills such as African building construction have been passed down. Some patterns of social, economic, and family organization are followed even today. One example is the social unit of the "Yard" in Kingston, Jamaica, which has its roots in West Africa. The "Yard" is a large house on a street with a maze of rented rooms and shared facilities at the back. Words from African languages are still in use. But perhaps the greatest survivals are African literature, music, and religion.

The tales of Brer Rabbit were published in the 1800s. There are now many great African-American writers, such as Alice Walker.

Stories with Meanings

Have you ever heard the Uncle Remus stories about Brer Rabbit and Brer Fox? They are all about animals that think, talk, and act like human beings and they are told using Southern African-American dialect of the 1800s. Children have enjoyed them for many years, but the stories are also important adult literature. For they are not only about animals, but also contain moral, political, and spiritual messages. In Africa, the West Indies, and North America, they still thrive. They have been enjoyed and studied in many parts of the world.

Many African stories were passed down through generations by word of mouth. This is called oral tradition and is an ancient way of teaching literature and history in many parts of Africa. Sometimes, stories are sung, accompanied by musical instruments – singers, called griots, learn their art from their fathers and grandfathers. It is a tradition that was continued in the Americas.

Dancing and Singing

Plantation owners did not forbid dancing and singing among slaves – they thought it helped people work harder. An African ring dance, where the dancers perform in the middle of a circle of musicians and singers, was one tradition that

African rhythms and moves are found in modern dance.

Jazz developed from the blues, a product of African music.

survived. Today, so-called American dance forms and rhythms, such as the conga, juba, rumba, and samba all have African roots.

Traditional African singing styles were used in the fields and mills. They were often in the form of call-and-response, where one person sang a line and the rest of the group chanted a reply. The rhythm was set to the movement of the work itself. It is thought that European sea shanties were developed from African calling songs.

Religious songs, perhaps more than any others, kept to African tradition. When Africans eventually took up Christianity, their own religious music was still strong. It greatly influenced how they sung Christian hymns. This is how North American gospel music came about, later influencing the musical styles of soul and rhythm and blues.

▲ Carnival is a mixture of Roman Catholic and African traditions. Different organizations make spectacular costumes in matching sets. Thousands of people dance and play music down the streets. This carnival is in Rio de Janeiro, in Brazil.

Lasting Beliefs

For 200 years, the majority of Africans in the Americas followed traditional religions. Although African peoples became mixed, certain ceremonies and gods were so strongly supported that they would not die out even when Christianity was accepted.

One example of this is the West African Yoruba thunder god, Shango. Today, Shango is also identified with John the Baptist, who baptized Jesus. In Bolivia, trances are achieved through taking part in Candomble, a ceremony based on African traditions and Roman Catholicism.

Converting to Christianity

Africans did not follow Christianity easily. Traditional religion had given them inner strength, and an organization from which to plan constant resistance

against their masters. In North America and the West Indies, the Church of England was viewed with suspicion, as was the Roman Catholic Church in South America. Both churches supported slavery. In the 18th century, the Archbishop of Canterbury, the head of the Church of England, had said that even if a slave chose to give his soul to God, the slave's body still belonged to his master.

But during the late 18th and 19th centuries, two Christian churches started to attract Africans. These were the nonconformist Methodists and Baptists. Africans found that some of their own religious ceremonies fitted in with those of the new Christian churches.

Above all, the white Baptist and the Methodist leaders treated slaves as equals. They spoke out angrily against slavery and used their churches to provide Africans with meeting places. As Africans became lay preachers and deacons, church became a place where the fight for freedom could be planned.

▲ This striking mural hangs in a Cathedral in Haiti. Here, Christianity grew separately after 1804, when ex-slave Toussaint L'Overture won independence for the island.

▼ An African-American preacher leads the service at this packed church in Washington in 1876.

The Road to Freedom

They were poorly paid, clustered together in bad housing, and suffered continual harassment.

William Wilberforce (born in 1759) became a British politician when he was only 21 years old. He fought for the abolition of the slave trade from 1787. In 1823 he founded the British Anti-Slavery Society.

Right from the beginning of the transatlantic slave trade, Africans had fought for their own freedom. As a protest, slaves often decided to work slowly or pretended to be sick. Many tried to escape and others organized rebellions. The punishments for those caught were extremely harsh. In North America, some slaves managed to flee to Canada. In the West Indies, runaways called Maroons, hid away from settled areas and tried to lead an African lifestyle.

Abolishing the Slave Trade

The anti-slavery movement was started by the Methodist and Baptist churches in Europe in the late 18th century. It was supported by European politicians and businessmen, partly because they now had interests in Africa itself.

The British politician William Wilberforce is often credited with ending the slave trade. His tireless petitions certainly helped to stop slave traders from operating in British colonies by 1808. But it did not stop other nations from trading in slaves. Neither did it stop slavery itself – in Brazil it ceased officially only in 1888.

It was the Jamaican slave rebellion of 1831 that finally stopped slavery in the British colonies. The violent way in which the rebellion was supressed caused public outrage in Britain. At midnight on August 1, 1838, 750,000 slaves became free, after 300 years of persecution and humiliation.

◀ **Maroons were able to build their towns in the remote green island hills of the Caribbean.**

▼ **A modern leader of the Ku Klux Klan preaches racism from behind a mask.**

▲ **The American general Colin Powell led the Combined Armed Services during the Gulf War. His views on military and foreign policy are widely respected.**

George Washington ▶ Carver, the son of slaves, worked his way through school to become one of America's finest scientists.

Freedom in the United States

In the United States, slavery did not end until the Civil War in 1865, when the anti-slavery northern states defeated the pro-slavery southern states. But life was still a hard struggle for African-Americans.

Africans who stayed in the south became sharecroppers. A sharecropper was given a piece of land, free of rent, by a white farmer. But in return, they had to give most of their crop to the farmer. This kind of bondage gave little more freedom than slavery. Further misery was caused by the racist organization called the Ku Klux Klan. African-Americans were abused and lynched by its members. The organization still exists today.

Other Africans took a risk and went north in search of work. They worked in mines and steel mills, on building sites and car plants – anywhere where there was a shortage of labor. They were poorly paid, clustered together in bad housing, and suffered continual harassment.

But despite poverty, oppression, and prejudice, the African-American community has produced notable scientists, educators, statesmen, military personnel, poets, musicians, and athletes, among others. Strong leaders have emerged, who have fought a long battle to gain equal rights for African-Americans in their country.

Africans in Europe

European nations treated their colonized peoples very differently.

The next large movement of Africans came in the 19th and 20th centuries. This movement was to Europe, and it came after European countries finally took over Africa itself.

The Race for Africa

By the end of the19th century, as the slave trade ended, African slave-trading states started supplying raw crops, such as palm oil, to Europe instead. European countries anxiously began to protect their own trading areas in Africa, taking over more and more African territory.

By the beginning of the 20th century, Britain,

By 1800, European influence in Africa had only just begun. Few Europeans knew what lay beyond the coastline. A century later, in 1914, the whole of Africa had been divided up between several European nations.

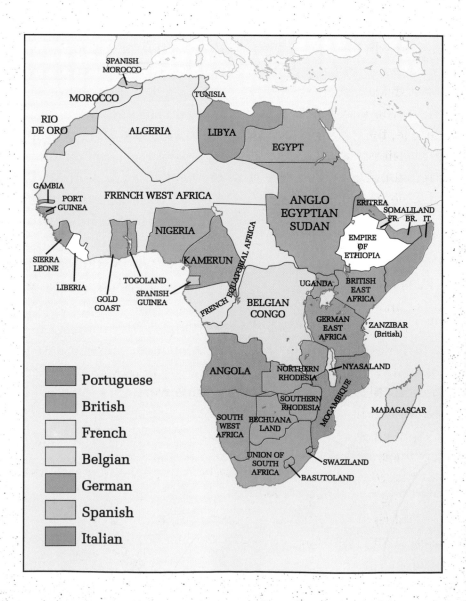

France, and Portugal had agreed to share the largest part of the continent, with smaller pockets going to Germany, Belgium, and Spain. During this colonial period, and even after African independence in the 1950s and 1960s, some Africans settled in the countries of their European rulers.

Africans in France

European nations treated their colonized peoples very differently. All of them saw Africans mainly as foreign labor, even though Africans were working in their own homeland. But to the French, Africans in their colonies were also considered Frenchmen and Frenchwomen. Higher education was offered to Africans in the French colonies, and students were allowed to study in France.

Africans settled in Paris especially, and although they suffered prejudice at the hands of some French people, there grew a large community of highly educated professional Africans. Many returned to Africa, giving their countries a better start when they eventually became independent.

An African Influence

French whites became aware of African culture. Prominent artists and writers began to respond to it. African sculpture was a major influence on the cubist style of Spanish artist Pablo Picasso, who worked mainly in France.

Today, there are many Africans in France. They have come mainly from poor independent countries such as Algeria, Morocco, and Senegal, which were once French colonies. Many were born and brought up in France. These people have added visibly to French life, with mosques, market stalls with African goods, and African restaurants. But French-Africans are suffering increasingly at the hands of violent right-wing political groups, who do not want Africans in France.

▲ Picasso's *Weeping Woman* was painted in 1937. The colors and shapes show the influence of African textiles and carvings. His sculptures share features of African bronze, stone, wood, and ivory carvings.

▼ Salif Keita is one of many musicians from French West Africa to have become popular performers in Europe. Their music is a blend of traditional and modern styles and instruments.

White and African sailors worked together on British ships for many years. Yet the treatment of Africans in Britain mirrored that of slaves in the Americas.

Africans in Britain

When Britain saw a trickle of Africans coming to their country during the colonial period, some whites reacted very strongly against them. It was not because this was the first time that Africans had settled in Britain. African workers, slaves and freed slaves, had made their homes there for hundreds of years, especially in Cardiff and Liverpool. By the early 20th century, a community of Somali railway workers had also laid down roots in Britain.

The racist attitudes of some British whites mirrored those of slave owners and followed British colonial policy toward Africans. There, Africans were seen as being fit only for work as laborers or as government clerks given simple tasks to keep the colonies running. Africans were treated like children – the colonial power, like a parent, gave them an exact framework in which to live. Unlike a parent, Britain did not encourage Africans to go "home" to the mother country to study or work. When they did, their welcome was often hostile, as was that given to the African-Caribbeans in 1950s.

The Promised Land

The settling of African-Caribbeans in Britain has been one of the greatest movements of African peoples in recent times. Britain gave up most of her West Indian territories in the 1960s. But before this, she had ruled a generally very loyal African-Caribbean community, who saw Britain as it had been taught to see it – as the mother country. Many

British African-Caribbeans now fill a huge variety of working positions in the U.K.

African-Caribbeans had fought and died for Britain during the Second World War.

After the war, Britain needed to rebuild its economy. The country was short of labor, so in the 1950s, the government advertised in West Indian newspapers, welcoming African-Caribbeans to work in Britain. For many of the islanders, this was a chance to escape from unemployment and poor wages and make a better life in the "promised land."

But the new arrivals soon discovered they had been misled. Many African-Caribbeans could not use their talents to the fullest. Qualified engineers worked as ticket collectors; experienced nurses washed hospital floors. Landlords turned away the new arrivals. African-Caribbeans were left with the poorest housing in the inner cities, where they daily faced racial prejudice. Many still face it today.

▲ Foods from the Americas and Africa are bought in Brixton market in London. Brixton is home to many British African-Caribbeans and newly settled Africans.

Changing Britain

Despite the hardship and the prejudice, the African-Caribbeans have become an important part of British society. Work can be difficult to find, but many have become highly qualified professionals. British African-Caribbeans have inspired music and poetry with new styles. They have influenced fashion and design. Their athletes from a wide variety of sports have raised national standards. Yet many African-Caribbeans still experience the hostility of some white Britons. They want to go back.

It is not just the older generation who are returning. Many young professional people, some of whom were born in Britain, see their future in the West Indies too. They do not feel that their contribution to Britain is appreciated. The loss to Britain in social, economic, and cultural terms has yet to be calculated.

◀ The Notting Hill African-Caribbean community proudly presents its carnival every year. Thousands flock to see the flamboyant costumes and parades.

27

Returning to Africa

The Pan-African movement encouraged pride among all peoples of African origin.

Ex-slaves were ► returned to Freetown, Sierra Leone, before the abolition of slavery by anti-slavery campaigners.

In 1821, a group of anti-slavery activists from the United States bought a piece of the West African coast. They called it Liberia – the "free land" – and shipped hundreds of freed slaves back to Africa. After abolishing the slave trade, Britain began to return Africans to West Africa. By the mid 19th century, 70,000 freed slaves had been settled in Sierra Leone, then a British-held territory. This was the first returning of Africans to their homeland on a large scale.

The Pan Africanist, Dr. W.E.B DuBois, was a professor of Greek, Latin, history, and economics. He also edited *Crisis*, a magazine which upheld the rights of African-Americans.

The African Identity

In the 19th century, "returning" for African-Americans and African-Caribbeans was part of a growing awareness of an African community in the Americas. The Pan African Movement, as it was called, encouraged pride among all peoples of African origin. Its leaders in the 19th and 20th centuries were African-American educator W. E. B. DuBois and African-Caribbean Marcus Garvey, who encouraged African-Americans and African-Caribbeans to set up their own businesses, banks, and insurance companies.

In the African colonies, the fight for independence had begun. Many of its leaders joined in the Pan-African movement. Léopold Senghor, a poet who later became the president of Senegal, firmly believed in the common identity of Africans all over the world. In his poem, *New York*, he expresses his joy at recognizing "Africanness" in Harlem, where many African-Americans live.

*Harlem Harlem! Now I saw Harlem! A green breeze of
        corn springs up from the pavements ploughed by the
        naked feet of dancers...
        ...And I saw along the sidewalks streams of white rum
        Streams of black milk in the blue fog of cigars
I saw the sky in the evening show cotton-flowers and
        seraphims' wings and sorcerers' plumes
Listen New York! Oh listen to your male voice of brass
        vibrating with oboes, the anguish choked with tears
        falling in great clots of blood
Listen to the distant beating of your nocturnal heart,
        rhythm and blood of the tom-tom, tom-tom blood
        and tom-tom*

▲ This 21-stringed instrument is the kora, played in far-West Africa. The young British African composer, Tunde Jegede, includes classical kora music in his orchestral work.

▼ Africans living along the course of the Gambia River were once taken as slaves to far-off lands. Nowadays, African-Americans come to the river in search of their past.

The "Back to Africa" movement declined as African-Americans and African-Caribbeans sought to strengthen their power within the white system – to get their own leaders into governments. But the movement was important. It gave people dignity and the will to fight for their rights. Today, African-Americans and African-Caribbeans, especially university lecturers, doctors, and artists, do go to Africa. Here, many feel freer and happier to contribute to the society in which they live. Some feel they really have come home.

Timeline

3,000 B.C.   Egyptian and Nubian empires emerge in Northeast Africa.

1000 B.C.-0   Evidence of large political and cultural units in West Africa.

800 B.C.-0   North African Carthaginians colonize Sicily and southern Spanish and Portuguese coastline.

0-A.D.500   Birth of Sudanic states between the Sahara and forest areas, and parts of Central Africa. Possibly more widespread than this.

By 300   Roman Empire and Christianity has spread in North Africa. North African Christian scholars, such as Saint Augustine, develop Christian ideas which help shape the Christian church.

634   The beginning of the spread of Islam by Middle Eastern Bedouin throughout North Africa. Moorish culture develops as a combination of Middle Eastern and African traditions.

711   The beginning of the Moorish empires in Spain and Portugal. Many North Africans move into Europe.

1491   Christian armies finally take over the last of the Moorish empire in Granada, Spain. Spain and Portugal become Christian kingdoms. The Portuguese start trading in African slaves from about this time.

1492   Christopher Columbus lands in the Americas and claims them for Spain. Explorers from other European countries follow. Beginning of European colonization of the Americas.

1500   The trade in slaves from Africa now established. It continues over 400 years – with its height in the 1700s.

1800   Increasing calls from concerned Europeans and Africans in Europe for the end of the slave trade.

1804   Once known as the French colony of Saint Dominigue, Haiti became the first truly independent Caribbean island in 1804. Ex-slaves, Toussaint L'Ouverture and Dessalines fought for the freedom of the island and are now remembered as heroes throughout the Caribbean.

1808   British slavers cease to operate.

1810   Beginning of repatriation of African freed slaves to parts of West Africa.

1838   End of slavery itself on British colonies – it still continues in others.

1865   American Civil War brings an end to slavery in the United States, but African-Americans still face poverty and racism. Many move from the southern states to northern cities to work in factories and transport.

1884-85   Berlin Conference in which European nations each express their wishes to take over certain parts of Africa.

1914-18   First World War.

1920   By this time, Africa has been divided up into colonies held by European nations, especially Britain, France, Belgium, and Portugal. A few Africans begin to study and work in European countries.

1920-50   The Pan-African movement led by W. E. B. DuBois and Marcus Garvey try to link peoples of African origin throughout the world – the "African Identity" develops.

1939-45   Second World War.

1950s   African-Caribbeans are invited to Britain to find work.

1950-60s   African and Caribbean countries gain their independence from European rule. Africans come to Europe in search of work and further education.

In the U.S., the Civil Rights Movement grows, led by leaders such as Martin Luther King. They fight to end segregation between white and African-Americans and for equal rights. Further laws against racial descrimination follow.

1990s   Some British African-Caribbeans begin to return to the Caribbean, finding Britain a difficult place to live. Africans continue to move to Europe. Some African-Americans and African-Caribbeans return to Africa.

Glossary

Baptists: members of the nonconformist Baptist church, which broke away from the Church of England in the 16th-17th centuries.

Candomble: a Bolivian religion that combines elements of African Yoruba and Roman Catholic beliefs and practices.

Carthaginian: the peoples and cultures of Carthage, a city on the North African coast. It was an important Mediterranean port throughout ancient times. It was part of the Roman and later Byzantine empires until the Muslims destroyed it in A.D. 698.

Church of England: the Church formed by Henry VIII in the 16th century. It broke away from the Roman Catholic Church. Its leader is the ruling monarch of Britain and the Archbishop of Canterbury is its highest bishop.

colonial period: in African history, the time when Europeans split up and ruled different parts of the continent – from the late 18th century to the 1960s.

culture: the social and economic customs, arts, beliefs, etc., of a particular group of people or the group of people who share these factors.

deacon: an officer of the church, or a member of the clergy, depending on the type of church.

Igbo: an ancient West African people, now part of the modern state of Nigeria.

Islam: a world religion begun in the 7th century by the Holy Prophet Muhammad (PBUH) and practiced by Muslims, who follow the Holy Prophet's teachings which are written in the Holy Koran.

lay preacher: a member of the church who performs some of the duties of a priest, including preaching sermons, but who has not been specially trained and subsequently ordained as a priest.

Marcus Garvey: a famous Jamaican-born Pan-Africanist and anti-racist activist (1887-1940). Most of his campaigning took place in the United States.

Methodists: members of the nonconformist Methodist church, founded by John Wesley, which broke away from the Church of England in 1795.

"middle passage": the middle stage of slave transportation, which was by ship.

migration: moving from one place or home to another, usually far away.

nomads: people who do not live permanently in one place and move regularly. They are often livestock farmers who need to find new pastures for their animals.

nonconformist: describes the various Protestant Christian churches that have broken away from the Church of England since the 17th century.

oppression: treating people with cruelty and injustice, so limiting their freedom.

oral tradition: history and literature passed down from one generation to the other through the spoken (oral) word, such as in stories and songs, rather than in written form.

Pablo Picasso: a famous modern Spanish artist (1881-1973) who, during a long and varied career, developed the cubist style of art. Cubist painters tried to show one object viewed from many different angles in a single picture.

prejudice: a judgment against someone without real cause – an opinion against someone or something which has been made without really knowing about that person or subject; someone who says "I don't like black people" is judging only by the color of the skin, and so is prejudiced.

professionals: people employed in the "professions," such as lawyers, doctors, teachers, where professional qualifications are needed.

right-wing: describes a person or an idea that is on the political "right," usually conservative. Extreme right-wing views can include some forms of racism.

Roman Catholic Church: one of the first organized Christian churches. The pope is its head and is based at the Vatican in Rome. Roman Catholics recognize the pope as God's representative on Earth.

sanitation: conditions for maintaining cleanliness, especially regarding the disposal of sewage.

trance: a state where a person is awake but appears to unaware of what is going on around him or her. In some religions, people believe that there is someone else's spirit inside them when they go into a trance.

Yoruba: an ancient West African people, now part of the modern state of Nigeria.

Index